WEAPONS & ARMAMENTS
OF THE MODERN
GERMAN ARMY
FULLY ILLUSTRATED

The Naval & Military Press Ltd.

Published by

The Naval & Military Press Ltd

Unit 5 Riverside, Brambleside
Bellbrook Industrial Estate
Uckfield, East Sussex
TN22 1QQ England

Tel: +44 (0)1825 749494

www.naval-military-press.com
www.nmarchive.com

THE BERGMANN MACHINE CARBINE—9 mm.

DETAILS: Overall length, 33in. Weight, 10¼ lb. (with sling). Magazine of the box type containing 32 rounds. Open type sights. Adjustment, 50-1,000 metres. Ammunition of the parabellum type. Either automatic or single shots can be fired.

STRIPPING AND REASSEMBLING: Depress the protruding upright catch to the left of the body, elevate the bolt lever and extract the bolt to the back.
Reverse the above procedure to reassemble the weapon, and pull the trigger.

TO LOAD: To cock this weapon, the bolt lever must be handled in the same way as the lever in a turning bolt action rifle. Push the magazine into its aperture on the right-hand side until fully home. To unload, depress catch, which will be found on magazine housing near side, and extract the magazine. Press the trigger.

NOTES: To set this weapon to "fire," pull the safety-catch back until the letter "F" appears. To set at "safe," push safety-catch forward until the letter "S" appears.
To fire gun automatically, pull the front trigger back until it operates the rear or secondary trigger, which immediately makes the gun automatic. To fire single shots, pull the front trigger lightly backwards, but not far enough to engage the second trigger.

9 mm. MACHINE CARBINES M.P. 40 & M.P. 38.

The M.P. 40 is the most recent of these two models, the original M.P. 38 having been primarily designed for use by paratroops, and now more or less out of date. Both models were notable owing to the entire absence of wood in their construction, and the folding shoulder rest common to both.

PARTICULARS: Weight, 9 lb. (without magazine). Weight of magazine, 23 oz. (when filled). Ammunition, 9mm. parabellum. Overall length, 33½in. (shoulder rest opened). Sighted for 200 m. (backsight, folding leaf type). Sighted for 100 m. (backsight fixed). Rate of fire, 520-540 r.p.m. (maximum). The feed is of the upright box type, containing 32 rounds. Six spare magazines and filler are carried in a haversack.

SAFETY: The weapon is "safe" when the letter "S" appears in the hollow behind the cocking handle groove.

STRIPPING: After making certain that the carbine is unloaded and uncocked, proceed as follows:—Withdraw and turn the locking pin underneath the body fore end. Press the trigger, at the same time rotating the body in an anti-clockwise direction. The barrel and

TO LOAD:

breech casing having now been extracted from the main body, withdraw the bolt and put back the spring by cocking the handle. (The spring is inside telescopic casing.) Put a loaded magazine into the aperture made to receive same and push in until it engages with a click. Pull back the cocking-handle. To unload the gun, simply depress the magazine catch and extract the magazine. Press the trigger.

INSTANT ACTION TO BE TAKEN ON STOPPAGES OCCURRING:
NOTES:

As for the Solothurn Machine Carbine.

To set the gun at "Safe," turn the cocking-handle into the small slotted hollow behind the cocked position, which is marked with the letter "S."
To fire this weapon automatically, push the traverse slide just behind and above the trigger group to the left. To fire single shots, push the slide to the right.

TO FIRE:

To extend the shoulder rest, press the thumb catch on the left and above the pistol grip.
Put a charged magazine into the feed by drawing back the cocking handle on the

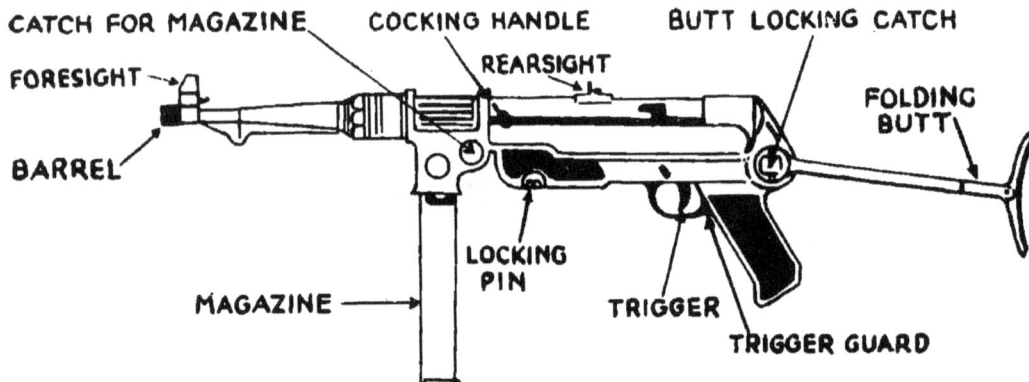

CATCH FOR MAGAZINE   COCKING HANDLE   BUTT LOCKING CATCH

FORESIGHT   REARSIGHT   FOLDING BUTT

BARREL

LOCKING PIN

MAGAZINE   TRIGGER   TRIGGER GUARD

AUTOMATIC MACHINE CARBINE SCHMEISSER M.P. 38 9mm. CALIBRE

left-hand side into the safety hollow. This exposes the feed. Next, detach cocking handle from safety hollow. The carbine is now ready for firing. Single shots are not allowed for.

THE STEYR-SOLOTHURN 9 mm. MACHINE CARBINE.

PARTICULARS: Weight, 10 lb. (approx.). Overall length, 32¼in. Bore, 9 mm. (.35in.). Speed of fire, 700 r.p.m. (maximum). Sighted up to 500 m. Feed, box magazine containing 30 rounds.

SAFETY: Safety catch to the fore of backsight.

STRIPPING: Take out magazine and make sure chamber is empty. Elevate the body cover by pressing the body cover catch. Draw back and extract cocking handle. Extract the breech block, together with firing pin and plunger. Firing pin will drop out if the cocking handle is extracted from the breech block by gently pressing and drawing out. The return spring can be taken out through the snare in the butt.

TO LOAD: Put a loaded magazine into the aperture made to receive same and push in until it engages with a click. Pull back the cocking-handle. To unload the gun, simply depress the magazine catch and extract the magazine. Press the trigger.

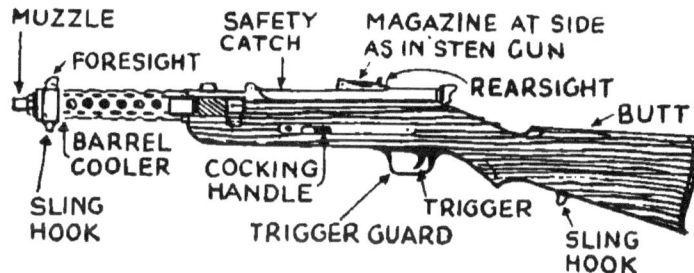

STEYR-SOLOTHURN AUTOMATIC CARBINE 9mm Calibre

INSTANT ACTION TO BE TAKEN ON STOPPAGES OCCURRING:

Cock the gun and exchange the magazine, after making certain that the magazine already fitted is correctly positioned. If stoppages continue, the gun must be stripped and examined for damage or burrs, cleaned and oiled.

NOTES:

Applied safety will be found to the fore of the backsight. To make "safe" push the safety-catch forward. To fire, pull the safety-catch back towards the sight. The safety device can be applied when the gun is either cocked or uncocked. A bayonet can be fitted to this weapon to the right of the barrel casing.

TO FIRE:

Put in a charged magazine. Draw back the cocking handle and put it back to its forward position. Adjust the shot device; for continuous fire, move back until the letter "D" appears; for single shots, move device forward until the letter "E" appears. To fire continuously, keep an even, heavy pressure on the trigger.

THE ERMA—9 mm. MACHINE CARBINE.

Similar in design to the Steyr-Solothurn, but with a safety device in the hollow behind the cocking handle —as in the M.P. 38.

PARTICULARS:

Weight, 9 lb. Speed of fire, 520 r.p.m. (maximum). Bore, 9 mm. (.35in.). Feed, box magazine containing 32 rounds.
For further details see the Steyr-Solothurn Machine Carbine.

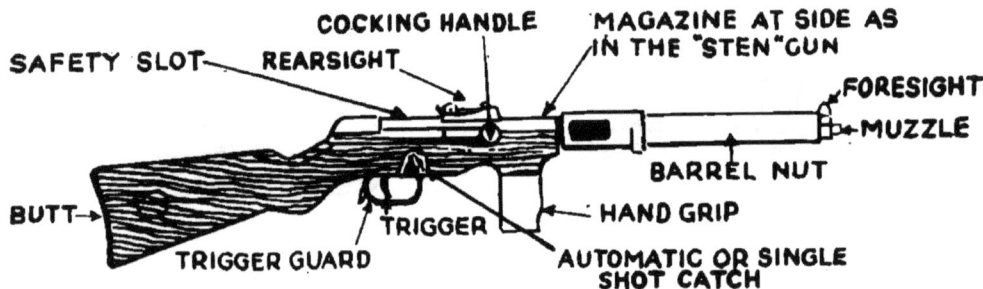

ERMA. AUTOMATIC CARBINE 9 mm. CALIBRE

THE NEUHAUSEN 9 mm. MACHINE CARBINE.

PARTICULARS: Weight, 9 lb. 2 oz. Bore, 9 mm. (.35in.). Speed of fire, 800 r.p.m. (maximum). Sighted, 1,000 m. Feed, upright box magazine type, containing 40 rounds.

It has been reported that a short-barrel model is in existence which weighs only 8 lb. 14 oz. and charged with only 30 rounds of ammunition, but full details are not, at the moment, available.

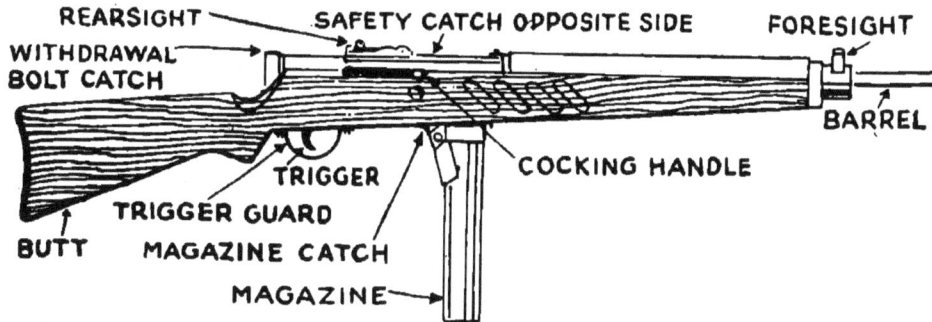

NEUHAUSEN AUTOMATIC CARBINE 9 mm. CALIBRE

THE SOLOTHURN 7.92 mm. MACHINE GUN 15.

This gun was designed primarily as an aircraft gun, but is sometimes used on the ground mounted on an A.A platform. This weapon will take the 7.92 mm. ammunition used by the British Besa Machine Gun.

PARTICULARS: Weight, 15 lb. 12 oz. Length, 42½in. (overall). Bore, 7.92 mm. (.31in.). Speed of fire, 1,000-1,100 r.p.m. (maximum). Sights: backsight, pillar type; foresight, ring type. Feed, 75 rounds contained in the saddle-type magazine. A bag is sometimes fitted beneath the ejector to hold spent cartridge cases.

SAFETY: Turn the safety arc until the letter "S" appears in line with the arrow marked on the body of the gun denoting "safe"; gun **must** be cocked to set at "safe." To set for "fire," turn arc until the letter "F" appears in line with the arrow mark.

STRIPPING AND REASSEMBLING: Position the safety-catch to the letter "F," then cock. Position safety-catch at "S." Turn the body extension group rather less than 45 degrees in an anti-clockwise direction by pressing down the safety-catch arc. Remove the body extension group by pulling backwards. Return the safety-catch to the letter "F." Put the bolt, face pointing downwards, on a firm base—though this base must not be hard enough to injure the mechanism—press the trigger, at the same time being careful to press the pistol grip downwards to overcome the upward force of the return spring. The firing-pin, firing-pin guide, bolt and return spring can now be extracted. To unscrew the cap at the end of the body extension group, the notched edges of the cap retainer must be loosened. This is done by putting a punch—such as a blunted nail—in the middle of the cap and hitting smartly towards the axis of the gun. Hold the fore end of the body extension in a downwards position, unscrew the large screw cap and take out. Extract the cap retainer. Press the trigger and move the trigger guard an inch or so backwards and take out. (It is as well to note here that the trigger guard may be a little stiff to move, in which case tap lightly with a wooden mallet—NOT a hammer.) Move the casing of the body extension backwards and extract the buffer and buffer spring. Take the barrel, barrel extension and locking nut from the barrel casing by elevating the ejector (found behind the magazine opening) and keeping it up while these parts are being extracted. Extract the muzzle attachment by elevating the pin and unscrewing. Take out the choke by gentle tapping with the wooden mallet until it drops off.

Reverse the above directions in order to reassemble the gun, being careful to note the following points :—

That the broader slot in the barrel extension is on top.

That the trigger is not pressed when replacing the trigger guard

TO LOAD Magazine. Three men are required to fill the magazine, one to hold the magazine in position, one to carry the strain by use of the loading keys, and one to insert the ammunition. If suitable support can be rigged up to hold the magazine firmly in position, this operation can be performed by two men only. First see that the safety-catch arc is set with the letter "F" aligned with the arrow. Then put the loaded magazine on the gun noting that the fore end of the magazine goes into the magazine opening first and exerting pressure on the back end of the magazine until the catch clicks home. This applies as in the Bren Gun. Lock magazine firmly in position by pushing the magazine catch

retainer over to the left. Pull the cocking handle back to its fullest extent.
To unload the gun, simply extract the magazine and then press the trigger.
Cock the gun, extract the magazine and press the trigger. See that the rounds of
ammunition have been correctly inserted by inspecting the mouth of the magazine.
If a round has become misplaced, take it out and continue firing after replacing the
magazine and cocking gun. If, after taking the above action, stoppages still occur,
insert a new magazine. If trouble still persists, strip, clean and well oil the mechanism
and keep a sharp look-out for damaged parts.
This gun can be used with R.A.C. 7.92 mm. ammunition.

NOTE:

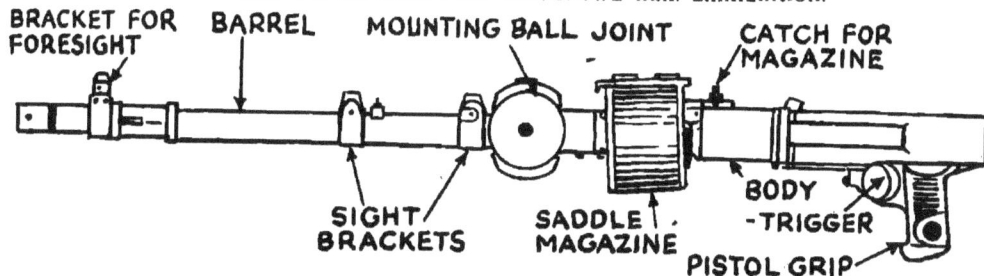

SOLOTHURN ANTI-AIRCRAFT TYPE M.G.15 MACHINE GUN 7·92mm Calibre

THE SOLOTHURN 7.92 mm. DUAL PURPOSE MACHINE GUN. (M.G. 34.)

This weapon can either be used on a light mounting as a Light Machine Gun or on a heavy mounting as a
Heavy Machine Gun, and is a standard weapon of the German Army.

PARTICULARS: Weight, 26½ lb. (light mounting). Length, 48in. (overall). Bore, 7.92 mm. (.31in.)
Speed of fire, 800-900 r.p.m. (maximum). Open sights up to 2,000 m., but with heavy
mounting and dial sight ranges up to 3,827 yards (3,500 m.) can be attained. Feed, of
the pliant metal belt type, containing 50 rounds. A container holding a spare 50-round
belt may sometimes be found attached to the left of the gun.

SAFETY:	A lever device manipulated with a spring catch maintains the "safe" or "fire" position. (Letters "F" or "S").
STRIPPING: (partial)	**To change the barrel.** Cock the gun and set to "safe." Press in the catch of the body to the left and beneath the backsight and give the body a full turn in an anti-clockwise direction. Take out used barrel and replace with new. Turn the body back in a clockwise direction until the catch of the body clicks home. Set gun to "fire." Pull the trigger and allow the cocking handle to move slowly forward. Further stripping is accomplished by the following method :—

(1) Elevate the foresight pedestal. Push in the catch underneath the fore-end of the barrel. Turn the mounting out of its groove and take away mounting.

(2) Open the feed cover by detaching the catch and extract feed block. Push in the pin at the end and to the right of the cover and thus take off the cover.

(3) Remove the butt by pressing the catch underneath and giving butt half a turn.

(4) To extract buffer housing first press the catch found at the rear and beneath the body of the gun and give housing a half-turn in an anti-clockwise direction. Take out return spring and, by means of cocking handle, extract the breech block.

(5) Taking off the body of the gun is the next operation. First press in the body catch beneath and to the left of the backsight pin. Give the body nearly a full turn in an anti-clockwise direction. Body can now easily be removed.

(6) Take the barrel from its casing. Pull up the catch to the fore of the foresight and unscrew the flash expeller.

(7) To extract the firing pin from the breech block, release the catch holding the sprung locking nut by gripping firmly and pulling smartly; then unscrew the nut which locks the firing pin behind the breech block conveyor. Put the stem of the breech block into the breech block conveyor back end so that that part of the firing pin locking sleeve which has been suitably manufactured to correspond with the formed aperture in the conveyor, fits snugly into place. Press down the breech block and rotate in a clockwise direction. Extract locking sleeve, firing pin and spring.

RE-ASSEMBLING:	Reverse the above directions, but NOTE (1) an audible click should result when the firing pin locking nut has been correctly screwed up. (2) When the breech block and conveyor are being fitted into the body of the gun, the guiding ridge on both must be in alignment, the trigger must be pressed, and the ejector pin completely advanced.

(3) The ridge on the feed arm must slide into the furrowed stud on the breech block conveyor when fitting down the feed cover.

TO LOAD:

Push forward the catch in front of the butt and lift up the cover. Place the loaded belt in position so that the right-hand cartridge engages with the stop to the right of the guide. Replace the cover and draw back the cocking-handle.

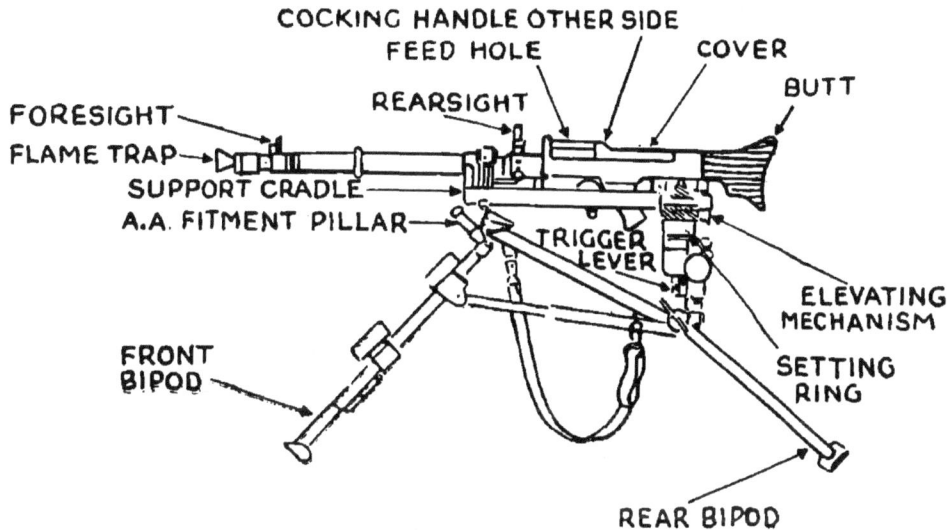

HEAVY MACHINE GUN M.G. 34. 7·92 mm. CALIBRE

TO UNLOAD:	Push the cover catch forward, lift up the cover and take out the belt. Press the trigger. Close the cover over the ejection opening; this cover is automatically open when the trigger is pressed.
TO FIRE (L.M.G.):	Compress the two legs of the light mounting and allow them to fall into position. Turn mounting back to front. A screw for height adjustment will be found between the legs. Elevate the sight columns and adjust the backsight for range by compressing the thumb pieces. Put the metal belt into the feed block. Cocking is attained as in the Bren Gun by drawing back the cocking handle and pushing it forward. If continuous fire is desired, pull the trigger from beneath (marked "D"); if single shots only are desired, pull the trigger from the top (marked "E").
TO FIRE (M.M.G.):	Mount gun on heavy mounting, which is sprung to take recoil. This mounting has an attachment for a dial sight and column to which an Anti-Aircraft connection can be attached. The trigger is operated by a lever, which is adjacent to the handle on the right-hand side of the elevating equipment. The heavy mounting has an uncommon automatic adjustment known as the "searching fire" device. This device automatically raises and lowers the angle of fire while the gun is in action. The device is operated by the recoil of the gun in its sprung bedding.

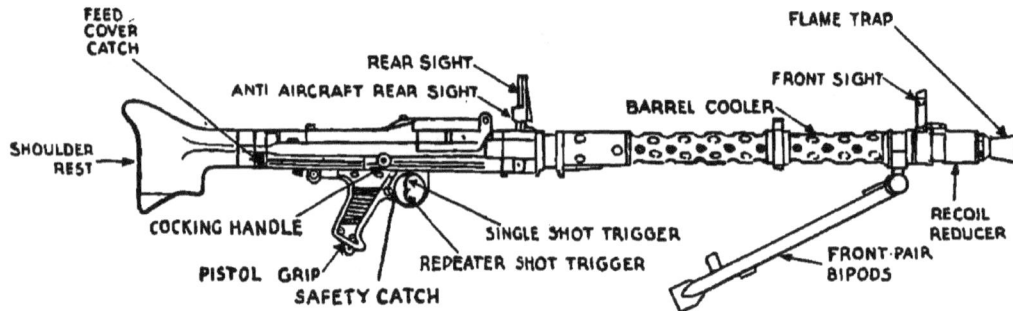

SOLOTHURN MACHINE GUN M.G. 34. 7·92 mm. CALIBRE

STOPPAGES: Immediate action must be taken to eliminate stoppages, as previously described in the case of other guns. In the case of the M.G. 34, take out the belt as previously described. NEVER raise the cover of the feed without first recocking the gun and hanging on to the cocking handle. Serious accidents can result if these precautions are not adhered to.

TO CLEAN AND OIL: Scrupulous cleanliness must be maintained and the gun kept well oiled. If cartridges are left for any length of time in a belt, the belt should be kept well oiled with paraffin. The ejection cover, which is automatically opened when the trigger is pulled, should on all other occasions be kept closed.

THE 7.92 mm. ANTI-TANK RIFLE.
(Models Pz. B. 38 & 39.)

These models have been developed by the Germans from a Polish anti-tank rifle, and are standard weapons in the German Army.

PARTICULARS: Weight, 27¼ lb. Length, 62¼in. (butt extended). Length, 50⅜in. (butt folded). Bore, 7.92 mm. (.31in.), specially enlarged to take a large cartridge case. Sights: Backsight of the "U" type and permanently adjusted for 300 m. Foresight of the blade type. Ammunition, A.P.T., of which there are two metal cartridge boxes, each holding 10 rounds and attached, one each side, at the front of the gun.

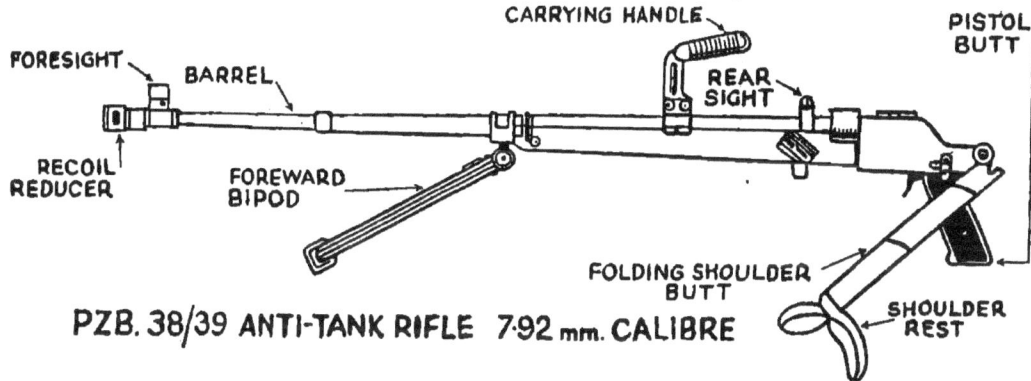

PZB. 38/39 ANTI-TANK RIFLE 7·92 mm. CALIBRE

SAFETY:	If catch exposes letter "S," gun set at safe; if catch exposes letter "F," gun set at "fire."
TO FIRE:	Mount gun on stand and extend the butt. Set catch to "F" (fire). Open the breech by a forward and downward movement on the pistol grip. Put a round of ammunition from a cartridge box into the chamber. close the breech by drawing backwards and upwards the pistol grip.

CARBINES AND RIFLES COMMON TO THE GERMAN ARMY.

NOTES.—These weapons are all manufactured on the basic design of the Mauser and may be divided into three distinct groups: (1) the short-barrel carbine which has an overall length of 43½in. and is known as model 98k. (2) The long-barrel carbine, which has an overall length of approximately 49½in. and is known as model 98b. (3) The rifle model 98, which is also 49in. in length and has the sling attached beneath it. These three types have a weight common to each of approximately 9 lbs.

PARTICULARS: (Carbines and Rifles)	Bore, 7.92 mm. (.31in.). Feed, upright box type magazine holding 5 rounds and loaded by charger. Ammunition, S.A.A. rimless 7.92 mm Sights: Foresight of the blade type; backsight stepped up from 100-2,000 m. and of the "V" type.
SAFETY:	To set for "safe," move over to the right or elevate until upright the safety catch behind the bolt. To set for "fire," move catch to the left. Safety catch cannot be manipulated unless the weapon is cocked.
EXTRACTING AND RE-INSERTING BOLT:	Draw back the bolt by pulling up the rounded knob. Extract the retaining-bolt lever on body left side and place bolt to the rear. To put back the bolt, first make certain that the extractor is completely over to the right of the bolt. Push the bolt forward after placing it in the body and at the same time extract the retaining-bolt lever. Press down the platform of the magazine, close the breech and pull the trigger.

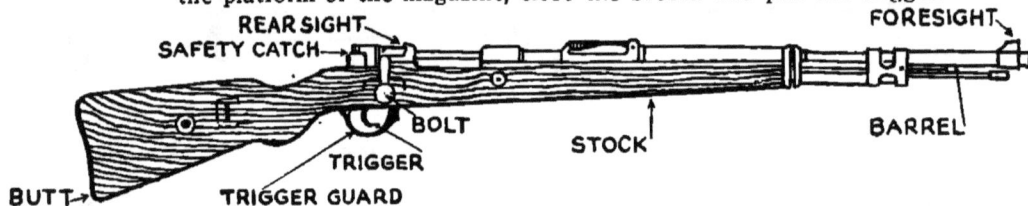

STANDARD MAUSER CARBINE 7·92 mm. CALIBRE

TO FIRE: Pull the bolt back to its fullest extent and open the breech. Place a charger upright between the guides. Press the cartridges down, the last one being free from the charger and retained in the magazine. Push the bolt forward and screw the knob down to its fullest extent.

S. Gr. W.34. HEAVY MORTAR (8 cm.).

NOTES.—Our own mortar operators should have very little difficulty in making use of any heavy mortars of this type which we may capture from the enemy as they are almost identical in general design and construction as the British 3in. mortar. The chief differences being the cross-levelling equipment which, in the case of the German model, turns the cross-levelling handwheel which, in turn, causes a pivoting motion of the elevating screw cylinder away from or towards the left support of the two-legged mounting, and so changes the cross level of the traversing equipment.

PARTICULARS: Weight of mortar, 125 lb. Weight of bomb, 7¼ lb. Charges, 4. Bore, 81.4 mm. (3.2in.). Range, 2,078 yards (maximum). *Sight, dial.

ASSEMBLY: Set the base plate on the ground in the desired position. Give the barrel half a turn. Arrange the two-legged mounting so that the elevating crank faces the barrel. Free the band holding the barrel in position. Rotate the elevating crank until one-third of the elevating screw can be seen. Replace the clamping band round the barrel. Lastly, attach the sight to the special holder and fasten up.

CHARGE: The first bomb(?) is fitted into the rear of the tail and in the centre. This constitutes charge No. 1. Charges Nos. 2, 3 and 4, if required, can be inserted between the vanes.

TO FIRE: Operate exactly as for the British 3in. mortar.

*The difference between the British and German dial sights is that in the case of the latter elevating and deflecting system is calculated in mils instead of degrees. If, during operations, line correction is required, say, to the right, i.e., the last round of ammunition fired having dropped to the left of the target, the additional deflection must be subtracted from the angle denoted on the deflection system; likewise, add the extra deflection if adjustment is required to the left—i.e., when ammunition is falling to the right of the target.

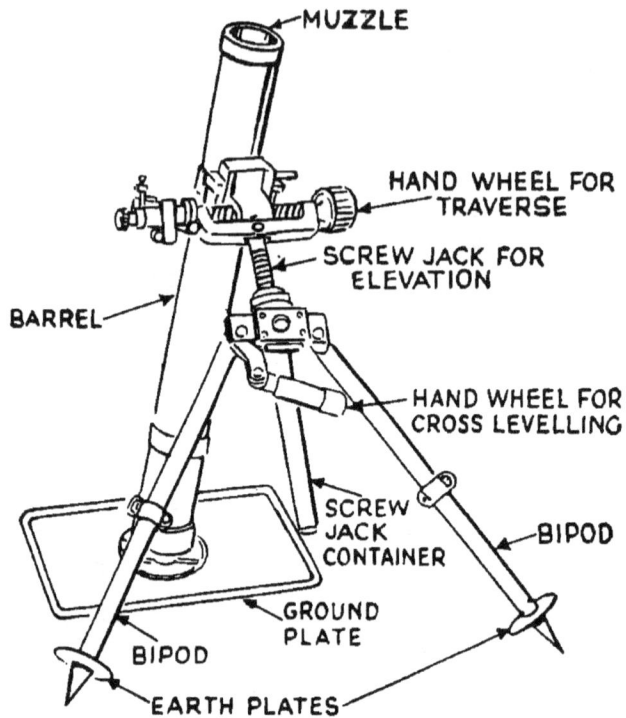

MUZZLE

HAND WHEEL FOR TRAVERSE

SCREW JACK FOR ELEVATION

BARREL

HAND WHEEL FOR CROSS LEVELLING

SCREW JACK CONTAINER

BIPOD

GROUND PLATE

BIPOD

EARTH PLATES

S Gr W. 34. HEAVY MORTAR
8 cm. CALIBRE

1 Gr. W.36—LIGHT MORTAR (5 cm.).

This is a standard weapon of the German Army and can be operated by two men. When in course of transit, one man carries the cross-levelling gear on his back and the other man the barrel and elevating screw. The weapon is designed to fire from high angles only—not less than 45 degrees, and is trigger fired and muzzle-loaded.

PARTICULARS: Weight of mortar, 31 lb. (total). Weight of bomb, 2 lb. Bore, 55 mm. (2 in.). Range, 568 yards (maximum). Speed of fire, 6 rounds in 8 seconds (approx.).

ASSEMBLY: Set traverse to 0 degrees. Withdraw hinge pin of barrel. Grip the barrel handle and set the elevating screw to lowest height. Put the barrel into its socket. Compress the catches and interlock with bottom end of elevating screw column, which will be found in front of traversing bracket. Insert the hinge pin of the barrel and elevate the range finder. Rotate the baseplate and use the white line marked on the barrel until correctly sighted on target. Press the baseplate firmly into the ground at an angle slightly inclined towards the target.

SIGHTING: Rough sighting is attained by pressing the lever to free the sliding collar, which enables the barrel to be elevated or lowered by manipulation of the barrel handle. For more accurate adjustments turn the elevating screw sleeve. Range is shown on an arc, scaled in metres (60-520), which is attached to the barrel and is read by means of an indicator fixed to the traversing bracket.

To adapt for line, move the baseplate after making sure that the traverse is at 0 degrees. Smaller adjustments can be made if necessary by using the traversing handwheel. On the left of the crossbar linking the two levelling handles together will be found a scale which is graduated to the nearest 10 mils and indicates amount of traverse.

A bubble fixed to the traversing bracket on the left of the barrel is used in conjunction with the two levelling handles, one on each side of the baseplate, to level the mortar. Turn handles to the right to move bubble backwards; handles to the left to move bubble forwards; to move bubble to the right or the left, move the handles inwards or outwards respectively.

TO FIRE: The layer lies flat on the ground face downwards, with his hands gripping the levelling handles and his forearms pressing on the baseplate. The loader, standing to the right of the layer, puts the bombs carefully into the muzzle of the mortar. Then, by slow and even backward pressure on the trigger, the loader fires when the order is given.

TO UNLOAD: Withdraw the hinge pin from the barrel. Fold the upstanding range indicator downwards and slowly elevate the breech end of the barrel and allow the bomb to slide gently
out into the hands of a member of the crew detailed to catch same.

MORTAR BARREL

ELEVATING SLIDING COLLAR

LEVER FOR RAPID RELEASE

SCREW SLEEVE FOR RAISING

HANDLE OF BARREL

LEVER FOR TRIGGER

HANDLE FOR LEVELLING

HANDLE FOR LEVELLING

OPEN COVER OF BUBBLE HOUSING

BASE

TRAVERSE BRACKET

HEAD OF BARREL HINGE PIN

HANDWHEEL FOR TRAVERSE MOTION

50mm CALIBRE LIGHT MORTAR

9 mm. LUGER AUTOMATIC PISTOL.

This is probably one of the most common of the German automatic pistols that may come into our hands and uses 9 mm. Parabellum ammunition only. This ammunition can be identified by the fact that it is approximately 1.14 inches' to 1.16 inches in length.

DETAILS: Weight, approximately, 2 lb. Length, 9in. Barrel length, approximately, 4in. Holds 8 rounds in a normal magazine.

STRIPPING: Take off the magazine and slightly press back barrel, then move downwards to the vertical position the thumb catch, which is found in the front of the trigger guard. Take out the covering plate and pull off to the front the recoiling parts of barrel and receiver. It is advised that no further stripping should be attempted as, in the event of damage being done to any parts, difficulty may be experienced in obtaining spares. To re-assemble, reverse the above instructions.

LOADING: Fit the mouth of a loaded magazine in the opening at the base of the butt and push it home until the magazine catch is engaged. Push upwards and to the rear with a sharp motion the two knurled knobs on the crank and let go. This will automatically cock the pistol and simultaneously the first round will have been fitted into the firing chamber.

UNLOADING: Take out by pushing in magazine catch, which is found to the rear of the trigger on the left- hand side of the pistol, then proceed with the same operation of pulling the crank backwards and let it go. This will automatically extract the round in the firing chamber. Finally, release spring tension by pulling the trigger.

SAFETY: A safety catch is fitted on the left-hand side of the body near the top of the butt. The safety catch can be placed in two positions—the more forward one being the "ready," and the furthest back is the "safe" position. Mechanical safety is ensured by the fact that, if the trigger is pressed when the action is not locked, the trigger bar cannot push in against the sear tail because the latter is then too far to the back owing to the fact that the recoiling portions are not fully forward.

NOTE.—This gun will utilise 9 mm. sten gun ammunition.

9 mm. MAUSER AUTOMATIC PISTOL.

DETAILS: Length, about 11in. Barrel length, approximately, 5in. Weight, 2 lb. 8oz. unloaded. Holds 10 rounds and utilizes 9 mm. Mauser ammunition, which can be identified by the fact that its length is approximately 1⅜in. These guns have open sights which are suitable for 50 to 500 metres.

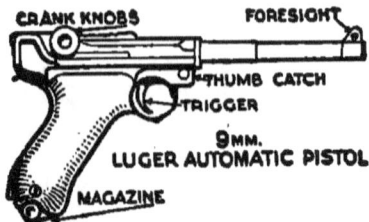

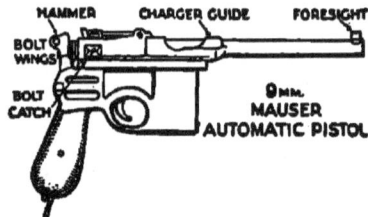

CRANK KNOBS | FORESIGHT
THUMB CATCH
TRIGGER
9MM.
LUGER AUTOMATIC PISTOL
MAGAZINE

HAMMER | CHARGER GUIDE | FORESIGHT
BOLT WINGS
BOLT CATCH
9MM.
MAUSER
AUTOMATIC PISTOL

FORESIGHT | HOLDING OPEN CATCH | SAFETY CATCH
HAMMER
LOCKING LEVER
TRIGGER GUARD
TRIGGER
9MM. WALTHER
AUTOMATIC PISTOL

STRIPPING: Press upwards the stud in the magazine base plate, then move the plate to the fore and take out the magazine platform and spring. Cock the hammer and push up the body catch which is beneath the base of the hammer; then it is possible to pull to the rear and clear of the body the hammer mechanism, barrel and barrel extension. These three parts can then be easily separated. Make certain when doing so that the body catch does not fall out of the hammer mechanism block. To remove the bolt from the barrel extension, use a penknife blade or small screwdriver to push in the back of the firing pin and give it a 90 degrees turn to the right. The firing pin can then be taken out. Finally, press to the fore the bolt catch on the right side of the barrel extension and pull it out to the right; this automatically releases the bolt return spring and then allows the bolt to be taken out to the back.

To re-assemble, reverse the above instructions.

LOADING: Pull to the rear the bolt; this causes the hammer to cock and permits the magazine platform to elevate, at the same time stopping the bolt closing again on an empty breech. Then fit a charger into the guides in the back of the breech and press the rounds into the magazine. Finally, take out the charger and the bolt will then automatically close at the same time moving the first cartridge into the breech ready to fire.

UNLOADING: Move the bolt to the back and front until it is held open by magazine platform, then hold the bolt back with one hand and push down the magazine platform; allow the bolt to go forward at the same time, seeing that no round has been left in the breech. Finally, press the trigger.

SAFETY: The catch is fitted at the side of the hammer on the left of the pistol body. When the catch is in its uppermost position the pistol is at "safety"; when in a horizontal position, the pistol is cocked and ready for firing.

SPECIAL NOTE: This make of automatic pistol is also supplied in a 7.63 mm. model and, to enable the user to distinguish them, all the 9 mm. patterns are marked with a large "9" on each side of the pistol grip.

THE WALTHER 9 mm. AUTOMATIC PISTOL.

This is probably the third most commonly used of German small arms that members of Home Guard units are likely to come across in the event of invasion taking place and, therefore, they should be in a position to understand the use and details of this weapon.

DETAILS: Approximately 8in. in length. Barrel length, approximately, 5in., including chamber. Magazine holds 8 rounds and uses 9 mm. parabellum type of ammunition. Weight about 2¼ lb. when loaded. This gun is supplied with fixed sights.

STRIPPING: First make sure that the safety catch is set at "SAFE," then take out the magazine and press back the slide with one hand and lift the "holding open" catch into engagement with the other hand; rotate the locking lever to the fore as far as possible (the locking lever is fitted on the left-hand side of the gun to the fore of the trigger guard). Next, whilst maintaining the slide under hand control, push in the "holding open" catch and move barrel and slide to the fore, then rotate the slide and barrel upside-down and press to the fore a small plunger at the back of the barrel assembly; this will automatically unlock the locking block and allow the barrel to be separated from the side. Finally, the locking block can itself be taken from the barrel. Do not try to effect further stripping as the mechanism is liable, in the hands of an inexperienced person, to suffer some possible damage.

ASSEMBLY: First refit the locking block in the barrel—making sure to see that the lugs on the locking block are truly in line with the barrel ribs. Then press the barrel assembly into the slide to its furthest extent, press the locking block with an upward motion into the locked position, then note if the hammer is to the fore when the gun is in the uncocked position, and that all moving parts that are in the body remain beneath the flat bearing surface level at the back end. Place safety catch at "SAFE" and hold locking block in the locked position, then press barrel and slide on to the body, pressing the slide as far back as possible and maintaining it there by lifting the "holding open" catch. Then rotate locking lever to the horizontal or locked position. Finally, push in the "holding open" catch and allow the slide to move to the fore; this will then enable you to insert the magazine.

LOADING: To remove the magazine, press back catch at the bottom of the pistol grip—this causes the magazine to come out sufficiently far enough to enable it to be held by the fingers and remove. To load the magazine, fit the base of each round to the fore of the magazine lips and push them in a down and backwards motion into place; then press the magazine back home into the pistol grip and move the slide back to its furthermost extent—finally allowing it to come forward under action of the return spring. It is of no consequence if the safety catch is set at "SAFE" or at the "FIRE" position as, in the former case, the hammer will already be in the firing position, and to actually start firing all that is needed is to set the safety catch at the "FIRE" position and pull the trigger, whilst in the latter case, the weapon is ready cocked and all that is required is to press the trigger. There is no necessity to cock the hammer on this model, as a double action hammer mechanism is used which enables the gun to be carried fully loaded but yet be set at "SAFE" with the hammer in an uncocked position, but it can be ready for action without having to waste time in actually cocking it. The "SAFE" position is when the safety catch is vertically downwards and the "FIRE" position is when the catch is set in the horizontal plane.

UNLOADING: Take out magazine and move back the slide to its furthermost extent so as to enable the removal of the round from the firing chamber and then allow the slide to move forward. This operation is carried out irrespective of what position the safety catch is in. Should the safety catch be in the "FIRE" position, then move it back to "SAFE"—this releases the hammer and removes tension from the springs.

SAFETY MEASURES: A safety catch is fitted on the left-hand side of the gun close to the back end of the slide; the catch can be moved from the "FIRE" position to the "SAFE" position, irrespective of whether the gun is cocked or uncocked. Should the pistol be uncocked, pressing the trigger will not fire the round, due to the fact that the hammer is stopped from moving rearwards sufficiently to be released; furthermore, the firing pin is automatically locked, even if the trigger is not fully retracted. Should the pistol be in the cocked position the hammer will be released and can come to the fore still without firing the round in the chamber because the firing pin is automatically in the locked position prior to the hammer hitting it. It is then automatically impossible to pull the trigger as it is in the fully retracted position.

GERMAN GRENADES. Brief Summary.

THE ENEMY PROBABLY KNOW ABOUT YOUR GRENADES, SO SOME DETAILS ARE GIVEN OF THEIR BEST KNOWN TYPES.

The best known of the grenades issued to the modern German Army at present are the Egg and Stick Hand Grenades, Models 24 and P.H. 39. These are designed for offensive use but rely on blast as against fragmentation, as they are constructed with thin metal cases. In the case of both, but particularly the "stick" grenades, the blast can be lethal, but generally the result is severe shock and, or, anti-morale effects.

THE "EGG" GRENADE.

Grenades of this type were originally used during the 1914-1918 war and for recognition purposes are painted standard German Service dark grey-green colour, the outer thin casing can be recognised by the outside having an elevated thin flange round its middle. In the centre of the grenade a pocket is fitted which holds the standard No. 8 German Service pattern detonator and also contains a 5-sec. delay flash cap. This pocket extends, approximately, to a depth of two-thirds of the actual grenade height.

HOW TO USE THE GRENADE.

To ignite the flash cap, there is a green knob approximately 5in. in diameter at the top of the grenade. When the knob is pulled the flash cap is fired by a wire operating link. The flash cap is fitted to the grenade body by means of either a wing or square nut.

PRIMING THE GRENADE.

First check that the detonator pocket in the centre of the body is clean and free from burrs; then release by unscrewing the protective cap from the detonator end of the flash cap. Take a detonator and check carefully to see that its open end is absolutely clean. **This is essential.** Carefully adjust the detonator on to the detonator end of the flash cap by slipping it over it. Finally, screw in the complete fuse by means of the square nut or wing nut on to the grenade body.

All that is now required to use the grenade is to simply release the green knob by unscrewing it and pulling.

RECOGNITION OF GRENADE.

The "egg" shaped container is approximately 2in. in diameter at its thickest point, by 3in. in length. The grenade weighs approximately ¾ lb., and the standard fuse fitted to this grenade has a 5-sec. delay action. The High Explosive filling of this pattern is very similar to gelignite.

It must be realised that a grenade of this weight can far out-range the British 36 M., further, the individual bomber can carry really large quantities, but whereas the 36 M. can be fired from a Cup discharger, this grenade, so far as is known, can be hand-thrown only.

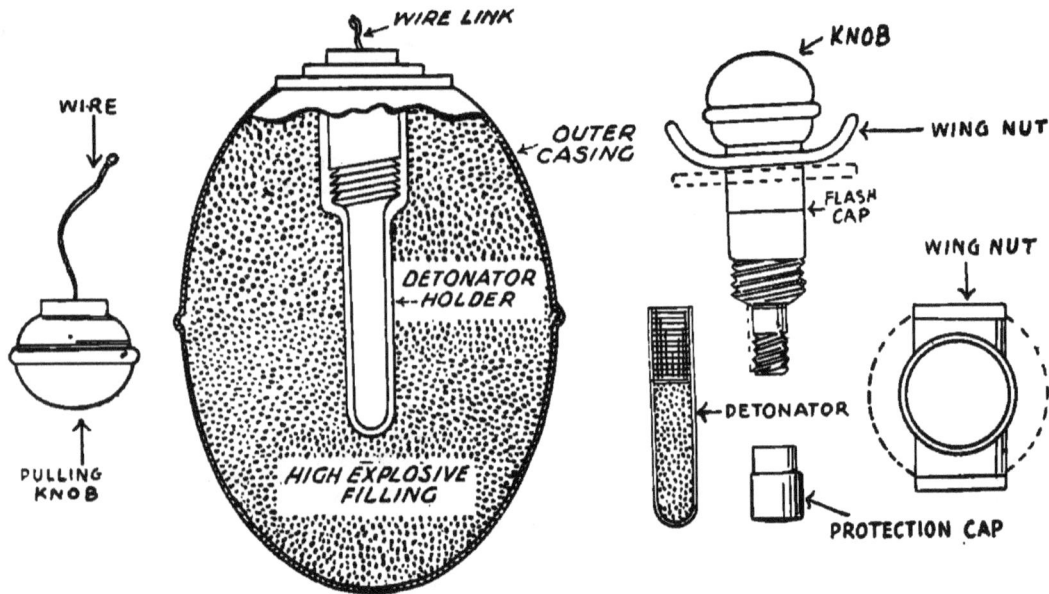

WIRE

WIRE LINK

KNOB

WING NUT

OUTER CASING

FLASH CAP

DETONATOR HOLDER

DETONATOR

WING NUT

PULLING KNOB

HIGH EXPLOSIVE FILLING

PROTECTION CAP

GERMAN EGG HAND GRENADE

THE MODEL 24 STICK HAND GRENADE.

This grenade can be recognised by its similarity in appearance to the well-known kitchen utensil, the "potato masher"; in fact, it was well known in the last war by this name. This type of grenade consists of a steel or iron head which contains High Explosive.

The explosive head itself is fitted to a wooden handle through the centre of which a double length of cord is run. One end of the cord is connected by a lead ball to the "friction" type Igniter Set, the other end of the cord is connected to a china bead which lies at the opposite end of the wooden handle in a small housing. This housing is covered by a screw cap to protect the china bead. When the grenade has been primed, all that is necessary to make the grenade ready for use is to unscrew the cap at the opposite end of the wooden handle to which the explosive head is connected and simply pull on the china bead.

This has the effect of setting off the friction igniter set which, in turn, explodes the detonator.

PRIMING THE No. 24 GRENADE.

Should grenades of this type be captured from the enemy, it will be found that they are usually without a detonator, and to prime them it is necessary to release the wooden handle from the explosive head by unscrewing it.

When this is done it will be seen that the metal end of the delay fuse is just exposed in the bore of the handle. Carefully fit the detonator into this end of the fuse, finally screwing the explosive head back on to the wooden handle, taking care that the threads do not get crossed. The grenade is now fully primed and ready for action. This grenade is fitted with 5-sec. delayed action fuse, and for recognition purposes is approximately 1ft. 2in. in total length and weighs just over 1¼ lb., the explosive weighing approximately 6 oz.

With regard to range, these again can be thrown further than the British 36 M., the length of the handle helping considerably. It will be noted that 6 oz. of H.E. is quite a high proportion of explosive for a grenade of this weight.

THE MARK PH. 39 STICK HAND GRENADE.

This pattern of grenade is very similar to the No. 24 mentioned above and functions in exactly the same manner. The only difference in its operation is that when the cap protecting the china bead is unscrewed, the cap itself is used to fire the friction igniter set. This is done by giving the cap a sharp pull, which automatically pulls the china bead beneath it and in turn pulls the cord and sets off the detonator. The difference in the outside appearance is that it is approximately 2in. longer than Model 24 and about 1 oz. heavier. The weight of explosive i slightly more than the No. 24, being a fraction under ½ lb. This pattern of grenade has a faster delayed action fuse which operates in approximately 4½ secs. As far as is known, the radius of effective danger when this grenade bursts is about 18 yards.

In spite of all the above grenades having a small danger area, they have this advantage that they can be thrown considerably further distances than this area, making it unnecessary for the thrower to have immediate cover available.

The enemy has an unpleasant, but effective, habit of fastening the heads of either 6 P.H. 39s or 24s round a complete "stick" grenade. The explosion of the complete centre grenade causes sympathetic detonation, making a formidable and concentrated demolition charge which is particularly effective when used against A.F.V.s, pillboxes, strong-points and in street fighting, as has been previously mentioned in using the British No. 73 and 74 S.T. grenades. The German method having the advantage of being a dual purpose grenade.

THE GERMAN HAND SMOKE GRENADE.

This grenade can be recognised by its likeness to the ordinary H.E. Stick grenade, but with the following difference: Instead of the normal grey-green H.E. explosive head being fitted, a smoke head is attached to the standard stick itself and the head is marked with a broken white band near its base. It also has stencilled on it the letters "Nb" in white.

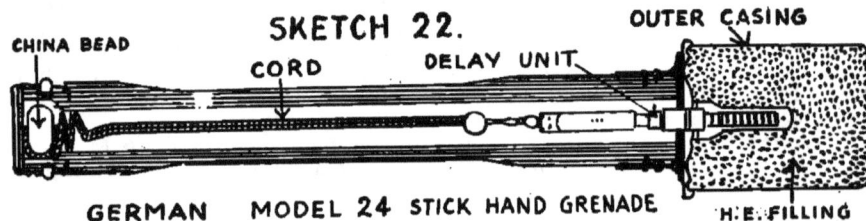

SKETCH 22.

CHINA BEAD — CORD — DELAY UNIT — OUTER CASING

GERMAN MODEL 24 STICK HAND GRENADE — H.E. FILLING

POLISH MACHINE GUNS.
Used by Germany.

After the brutal attack of the Germans on Poland, it is fair to assume that many weapons of the Polish Army fell into their hands, including the Light and Heavy M.G.s. The M.28 (L.M.G. .79 cm.) has a weight of 22 lb., fire 600 r.p.m., and has a magazine holding 20 rounds. The M.30 (.79 cm. L.M.G.) has a weight of approximately 103 lb. (with mounting), fires at the rate of 600 r.p.m., has a belt type of feed, and is water-cooled.

Polish Mortars are also undoubtedly being used by the German Army. Details of these are as follows:—

(1) The 4.6 cm. M.30 weighs approximately 15 lb., has a range of about 765 yards, and projects a bomb weighing 1½ lb. (2) The Stokes-Brandt Mortar (8.1 cm.) weighs 129 lb., has a range of 3,200 yards, and projects a bomb weighing 7 lb. (approx.).

As the Polish weapons fell into the hands of the Germans, so the French weapons followed suit. Details of the French mortar are as follows:—The 8.1 cm. French Mortar is almost identical in design to the German 8.1 cm. Mortar, and for this reason alone is undoubtedly being used by the Germans.

The Polish Anti-Tank Rifle weighs approximately 19½ lb., has an overall length of 6¼ ft., and a .79 cm. bore. This weapon is fired as an ordinary rifle—i.e., from the shoulder, fires single shots, and is fitted with a special device for taking the recoil.

It can safely be assumed that the following French A/T. guns are also being utilised by the Germany Army: The 7.5 cm. A/T. gun, is believed to fire at the rate of 12 r.p.m. Projects a 14 lb. A.P. shell. Penetration is unknown.

The 4.7 cm. A/T. gun (M.39) fires at the rate of 20 r.p.m. Projects a 3½ lb. A.P. shell, which has a penetration of 80 mm. at 220 yards at an angle of 15 degrees.

The 2.5 cm. Hotchkiss A/T. gun fires at the rate of 20-25 r.p.m. Projects a 7 lb. A.P. shell, which has a penetration of 60 mm. at 100 yards range when fired at normal.

The 2.5 cm. Puteaux A/T. gun is similar to the 2.5 Hotchkiss A/T. gun in respect of performance.

CHARACTERISTICS OF GERMAN GLIDERS.
THE GERMAN GLIDER D.F.S. 230.

DIMENSIONS.		
Span	72 ft. (approx.)
Length	36 ft.
Weight (empty but including equipment)	1,800 lb.
Maximum load	2,850 lb.
Usual load	2,600 lb.
Maximum flying weight	4,600 lb.
Usual flying weight	4,400 lb.

The fuselage of this glider is constructed of steel, while the wings are made of wood only. Its wheels are detachable and on operational flights are entirely dispensed with. Flaps are fitted to the wings which, when elevated, allows the angle of glide to be steepened. When the glider carries its full complement of men—ten in number, including pilot—the space inside is somewhat restricted. Six of these men sit facing the front and four sit facing the rear. A door at either end of the glider enables the men to enplane and deplane very rapidly. Being engineless, an accumulator is attached to the nose of the plane to operate the landing light and navigation lights. The instruments in the interior are luminous and consist of a compass, an altimeter, a bank and turn indicator, and also a rate of climb indicator. For armament the glider is supposed to have one L.M.G. attached outside on the starboard side, which the man sitting in seat No. 2 is said to operate through a small slot in the fuselage when the glider comes in to land on enemy territory.

THE GERMAN GLIDER—GOTHA 242.

DIMENSIONS.	Span	...				79 ft.
	Length	...	...	...	...	52½ ft.

This glider is considerably larger than the D.F.S. 230, but is similar in construction, the wings, tail and boom being made entirely of wood and the fuselage of tubular metal. The three wheels are detachable, but can be used to land as an alternative to the three skis which are also fitted for the purpose of landing. The rear part of the fuselage can be lifted for the purpose of loading and special ramps are carried for this purpose. When raised the aperture thus provided measures approximately 7ft. x 6ft. This machine is used for the transport of freight as well as troops.

The glider is operated by two pilots, and is dual controlled.

Armament consists usually of four L.M.G.s, two fore and two aft, though sometimes these may be supplemented by two on each side.

Being a larger glider than the D.F.S. 230, it has a somewhat more elaborate equipment, including an inter-communicating telephone with the pilot, of the towing aeroplane, which is operated by means of an accumulator, also a container holding ballast of weight up to approximately 920 lb.

This glider carries 21 men with their full equipment in addition to the two pilots. If used as a freight carrier, can be loaded as follows :—

Space for stowage	...	...	...	20 ft. x 8 ft. x 6½ ft.
When empty	...	...	...	7,250 lb. (including armament).
Maximum load ... - ...	...	...	...	5,300 lb.
Maximum flying weight	...	...	...	12,540 lb.
Gliding speed (maximum)	...	...	...	180 m p.h.
Maximum towing speed	...	...	...	149 m p.h.

The glider is usually towed by means of a steel cable of varying lengths (100-300 yds.) attached to a Ju. 52.

Although supposedly easy to handle, these gliders will not stand up to steep banks or any type of aerobatics.

THE GERMAN MERSEBURG GLIDER.

This glider is larger than either of the foregoing, having a span of 175 ft. and a length of 94 ft. Few details are available at the present time, but it is estimated that its probable carrying capacity is somewhere in the region of 20,000 lb. (max.). This machine would be quite capable of taking the Pz. Kw. II tank, which weighs 9 tons. One Ju. 52, however, would be insufficient to tow a 20,000 lb. load, so it must be assumed that more than one towing plane would be utilised.

THE GERMAN GOLIATH GLIDER.

This glider is the largest of the lot, having a wing span of approximately 270 ft. It is supposed to be capable of carrying 140 men or about 16 tons of freight. This glider would require three Ju. 52s to tow it. Very few details are available about this glider.

German Light Armoured Car, Sd. K.F.Z. 13. Weight 2½ tons. Speed 45-50 m.p.h. Height 5' 0". Length 14' 0". Width 5' 6". Crew 2 or 3. Armed with 1 Medium M.G. How to recognise: Open top turret. 4 wheels. Front bonnet as civilian type motor car. Mudguards fitted. Spare wheel fitted on back. Looks similar to private car in many ways.

German Heavy Armoured Car, Sd. K.F.Z. 231. Weight 9 tons. Speed 30 m.p.h. Height 8' 0". Length 19' 3". Width 6' 6". Crew 4. Armed with a Medium M.G. and a 20 m.m. Heavy M.G. How to recognise: 8 wheels. Low turret mounted to the fore. Very snub-nosed. Stream-lined body. Rear body slopes towards the ground. Fitted with semi-silent engine and often used as Commander's vehicle. Occasionally fitted with frame aerial. Front view almost diamond shaped and appears top-heavy.

This is a Model K.G.Z. 232 (8 RAD) when fitted with aerial.

German Light Medium Armoured Car, Sd. K.F.Z. 221. Weight 4 tons. Speed 45 m.p.h. Height 5' 6". Length 15' 9". Width 6' 6". Armed with an Anti-Tank Rifle and a Light M.G. Crew 2. How to recognise: 4-wheel chassis. Turret with open top sometimes fitted with square grid pattern aerial. Mudguards fitted fore and aft. Body slopes downwards back and front.

German Assault Gun fitted on Pz. Kw. 3. Tank chassis armed with either short or long-barrelled 75 m.m. gun. How to recognise: Very low, squat, stream-lined shape—both sides and front view. Driver controls from left hand side. Fitted with 6 small bogie wheels and large driving sprocket. 3 very small jockey wheels each side.

German Light Armoured Car, Sd. K.F.Z. 222. Weight 4½ tons. Speed 35 m.p.h. Height 7' 6". Length 15' 6". Width 6' 3". Crew 3. Armed with a Medium M.G. and a 20 m.m. Heavy M.G. How to recognise: 4 wheels with mudguards. Body slopes to ground back and front. Semi-stream-lined hull. Front view of body almost diamond shaped.

Side view should show spare wheel mounted on body centre.

German Mark II. Light Armoured Car. Height 6' 3". Length 15' 0". Width 6' 0". How to recognise: Completely welded armoured beetle-shaped body, giving very similar appearance fore and aft. Engine fitted rear. Small, flat open top turret protected by metal grid fitted in vehicle centre and mounting 1 light gun. Prominent bumpers. Engine fore part. Bodyslopes from above mid-line to axle level. Mounting spare wheel each side. Front view shown body overhanging the 4 wheels in the centre.

German Medium Armoured Car, Sd. K.F.Z. 231. Previously known as A.S.P.4. Weight 6½ tons. Speed 32 m.p.h. Height 7' 6". Length 18' 6". Width 6' 0". Crew 4. Armed with one M.G. and one 20 m.m. heavy M.G. How to recognise: 6 wheels with very long bonnet sloping to the fore. Bonnet front stream-lined. Squat turret. 2 rear wheels each side have common mudguards. Sometimes fitted with grid umbrella type aerial (as in Sketch).

This is a model K.F.Z. 232 when fitted with grid-type aerial.

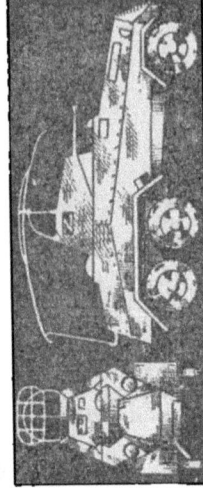

German Light Tank—Ex. Czech S.11 A. Lt. 2S. New No. 1 Pz. Kw. 35 (t). Weight 10½ tons. Speed 20-25 m.p.h. Height 7' 4". Length 15'. Width 7'. Crew 4. Armed with a 37 m.m. gun and 2 M.G.'s. How to recognise: Rectangular turret face for gun mantlet with 2 M.G.'s fitted with ball mounting. Sprocket and idler wheels have large flanges. Twin bogies with 4 sets of wheels each and 1 independent wheel on each side. 4 very small jockey wheels. Aerial mast left side and to the fore of turret. Watch-out cupola left side middle of turret.

German Light Tank, Pz. Kw. 1.

How to recognise: Turret set over to the right when seen from front. Gun mantlet rounded. 5 bogie wheels unevenly spaced each side with girder outside linking suspension. 4 very small jockey wheels. Weight 5.7 tons. Speed, Road, 32 m.p.h.: radius of action 95 miles. Engine 90/100 h.p. Dimensions: Length 12' 6". Width 5' 7". Height 5' 7". Ground clearance 12". Performance: Trench 4' 7". Step 1' 2" (approx.). Water 2'. Gradient 45°. Suspension: 5 bogie wheels. Combination of rocker and semi-elliptical springs and independent coil springs. Crew 2. Armour basis: Front 18 mm., Turret 18 mm. Remainder 14 mm. Armament: Two 7.91 mm. M.G.'s coaxially mounted. Ammunition carried. 2,000 rounds. Fuel, Petrol. Communication: External, wireless transmitter.

German Maybach Light Tank. "Leger." Pz. Kw. 1.

Height 5' 6". Length 13' 0". Width 6' 10". **How to recognise:** Five equally spaced bogie wheels with horizontal outer girdle. Central high super-structure with round turret centrally placed. Similar in appearance to Pz. Kw. 1. No further details available.

On later models has spaced armour on gun mantlet and in front of driver and hull gunner: also dish-shaped sprocket.

German Light Tank.—Ex. Czech Lth.

Now called Pz. Kw. 38 (t). Weight 9½ tons. Speed 36 m.p.h. Height 7' 3". Length 15' 4". Width 7' 0". Crew 4. Armed with 2 M.G.'s and one 37 m.m. gun. **How to recognise:** 4 very large bogie wheels practically contacting track top. Very heavy riveted turret with watch-out cupola on left hand side. Gun mounting has rectangular lace on turret. Aerial mast left hand side to the fore of turret.

German Light Medium Tank Pz. Kw. 2.

How to recognise: Streamlined, squat turret with long-barrelled heavy M.G. Large driving sprocket at front. 5 bogie wheels each side, independently sprung. Aerial mast left hand side behind top turret.

Weight 9 tons. Speed, Road, 25 m.p.h.: radius of action 125 miles. Engine: Maybach. 6 cylinder. Dimensions: Length 15' 4". Width 7' 5". Height 6' 5". Ground clearance 11". Performance: Trench 4' 11". Step 1' 11", Water 2' 6". Gradient 45°. Suspension: 5 independent elliptically-sprung bogie wheels. Crew 3. Armour basis: Front, 38 mm. gun mounting and front of turret. Superstructure: front, 40 mm. Remainder, 15-18 mm. Armament: One 2 c.m. H.M.G.: one L.M.G. coaxially mounted. Ammunition carried. 224 rounds for H.M.G. Fuel, Petrol. Communication: Internal, telephone: External, wireless transmitter. Observation: 8 periscopes for gunner in cupola.

German Medium Tank, Pz. Kw. 3.

How to recognise: Very large front driving sprocket. Some models fitted with very long gun barrel overhanging front of hull. Low streamlined turret with rear watch-out cupola. 3 sets of 2 independently sprung small bogie wheels each side. Front view, turret sides slope inwards towards the top. Weight 18-20 tons. Speed 28 m.p.h.: radius of action. 75-100 miles (estimated). Engine: Maybach V. 12 cylinder. 320 h.p. Dimensions: Length 17' 8". Width 9' 9". Height 7' 9". Ground clearance. Trench. 6' to 7'. Step 3'. Water 2' 11" (estimated). Suspension: 6 independent bogie wheels. Crew 5, consisting of driver, hull gunner/wireless transmitter operator, commander, gunner and loader. Armament: One 5 cm. Q.F. gun. Gun mounting 70 mm., front superstructure 60 mm., rear deck 20 mm., remainder 20 mm. Ammunition carried, 100 rounds for Q.F. gun: 2,000 rounds for one 7.91 mm. M.G. coaxially mounted: one 7.91 mm. M.G. in hull. Communication: Internal, telephone: External, wireless transmitter. Observation: All-round periscopes.

German Medium Tank, Pz. Kw. 4.

Some models have large gun fitted with very long barrel which has a globular muzzle brake overhanging the hull. **How to recognise:** 8 small bogie wheels with large front driving sprocket. Low streamlined turret with watch-out cupola on turret rear, centrally placed. Aerial mast fitted right hand side towards turret fore. Weight 22 tons. Dimensions: Length 19' 2". Width 9' 5". Height 8' 7". Ground clearance 1' 2". Performance: Trench 6' to 7'. Step 3'. Water 3' (estimated). Suspension: 8 small bogie wheels in pairs with cantilever springs. Crew 5. Armour basis: Sides of hull superstructure 40 mm., front plates 60 mm., rear deck 10 mm., remainder 20 mm. Armament: One 7.5 cm. gun: one 7.91 mm. M.G. coaxially mounted: one 7.91 mm. M.G. in hull. Ammunition carried: 85 rounds H.E. and A.P. for gun, 2,000 rounds for M.G.'s. Fuel: 103 gallons of petrol. Communication: Internal, telephone: External, wireless transmitter. Observation: All-round periscopes.

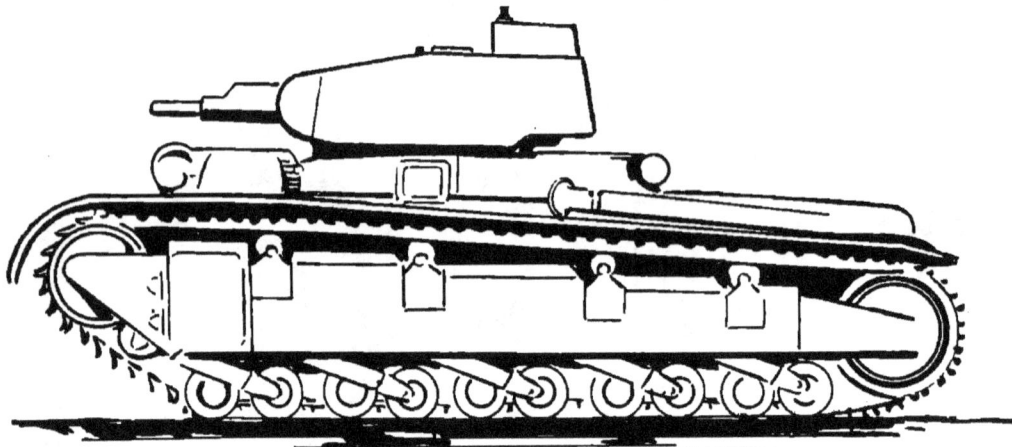

GERMAN HEAVY TANK P2.Kw5. FULL DETAILS IN TEXT MATTER

GERMAN Pz. Kw. V Heavy Tank.

Weight	36 tons.
Speed	Road: 10-13 m.p.h.; radius of action: 75-85 miles.
Engine	350 h.p.
Dimensions	Length: 25-26ft.
	Width: 9ft.
	Height: 10-11ft.
Performance	Trench: 11ft. 6in.
	Step: 4ft. 7in.
	Water: 3ft. 4in.

Suspension	...	...	11 small bogey wheels protected by skirting.
Crew	...	... ...	7-8.
Armour basis	...	...	2in. (vulnerable points possibly 4in.).
Armament	...	...	One 7.5 cm. gun; one 3.7 cm. Q.F. coaxially mounted; three L.M.G.s (1 in main turret, 1 in each subsidiary turret)
Communication		...	Internal: telephone. External: wireless transmitter.

BRIEF DETAILS OF GERMAN TIGER TANK.

Weight	62 tons.
Length to end of gun	27ft.
Length of hull	19ft.
Width overall	12ft. 8in.
Width (from middle of tracks)	10ft. 5in.
Height to top of cupola	9ft. 5½in.
Height to top of superstructure	5ft. 3in.
Length of gun from mantle to end of muzzle brake	12ft. 7in.
Main armament	88 mm. gun.

No available illustration of this A.F.V.

Characteristics of French and Czech Tanks.

FRENCH.

	Weight.	Dimensions.	Armour.	Armament.	Speed.	Crew.	Performance.	Communication.
Char "B" Heavy Tank.	32 tons.	21' 0" long. 8' 0" wide. 9' 3" high. 1' 6" belly clearance.	Front : 60 mm. Sides : 60 mm. Top : 20 mm.	1 75 mm. Gun. 1 47 mm. Gun. 2 M.G.'s	15 m.p.h. 100 miles radius.	5	9' 0" trench crossing. 3' 9" step. 4' 9" water. 40° gradient (max.).	W/T. & R/T.
Somua S. 40 Medium Tank.	19 tons.	18' 0" long. 6' 9" wide. 8' 9" high. 1' 3" belly clearance.	Front : 40 mm. Sides : 40 mm. Top : 15 mm.	1 47 mm. Gun. 1 M.G.	30 m.p.h. 125 miles radius.	3	7' 9" trench crossing. 3' 0" step. 3' 3" water. 40° gradient (max.).	W/T & R/T.
Hotchkiss H. 39 Light Tank.	12 tons.	15' 0" long. 7' 0" wide. 7' 2" high. 1' 0" belly clearance.	Front : 40 mm. Sides : 40 mm. Top : 18 mm.	1 37 mm. Gun. 1 M.G. coaxial in turret.	25 m.p.h. 120 miles radius.	2	5' 0" trench crossing. 2' 6" step. 2' 6" water. 40° gradient (max.).	Flag.

CZECH.

	Weight.	Dimensions.	Armour.	Armament.	Speed.	Crew.	Performance.	Communication.
L.T.H. Light Tank (Pz. Kw. 38 t.).	9.5 tons.	15' 4" long. 7' 0" wide. 7' 3" high. 1' 3" belly clearance.	Front : 25 or 50 mm. Sides : 15 mm. Top : 10 mm.	1 47 mm. Gun. 1 7.92 mm. M.G. coaxial in turret. 1 7.92 mm. M.G. in hull.	36 m.p.h. 100 miles radius.	4	6' 6" trench crossing. 2' 9" step. 3' 0" water. 30° gradient (max.).	W/T.
L.T. 35 S.11 A. Light Tank. (Pz. Kw. 35 t.).	10½ tons.	15' 0" long. 7' 0" wide. 7' 4" high. 1' 0" belly clearance.	Front : 28 mm. Sides : 24 mm. Top : 12 mm.	1 37 mm. Gun. 1 7.92 mm. M.G. coaxial in turret. 1 7.92 mm. M.G. in hull.	20 m.p.h. 75 miles radius.	4	6' 6" trench crossing. 2' 6" step. 2' 6" water forded. 30° gradient (max.).	
R.I. Light Tanks ...	3½ tons.	10' 0" long. 7' 0" wide. 5' 6" high. 1' 0" clearance.	Front : 14 mm. Sides : 8 mm. Top : 8 mm.	1 37 mm. Gun. 1 M.G.	25 m.p.h.	2	5' 0" trench crossing. 2' 0" step. 2' 6" water. 45° gradient (max.).	
S.I. Light Tank ...	4 tons.	8' 6" long. 6' 0" wide. 4' 6" high. 9" clearance.	Front : 14 mm. Sides : 8 mm. Top : 8 mm.	1 37 mm. Gun. 1 M.G.	25 m.p.h.	2	5' 0" trench crossing. 2' 0" step. 2' 6" water. 45° gradient (max.).	

Data Chart of A.F.V.'s and Armaments of a Panzer Division.

	A.-Tk. Bn.	Div. Sigs. Bn.	Engineer Bn.	Mot. A.A. Bn.	Tank Regt.	Recce. Unit.	Lorried Inf. Bn	Div. Arty
Pz. Kw. VI. (" Tiger ") ...	—	—	—	—	?	—	—	—
Pz. Kw. V.	—	—	—	—	?	—	—	—
Pz. Kw. II.	—	—	—	—	69	—	—	—
Pz. Kw. III.	—	—	—	—	102	—	—	—
Pz. Kw. IV.	—	—	—	—	30	—	—	—
Lt. Armd. Cars	—	—	—	—	—	38	—	—
Hy. Armed Cars	—	—	—	—	—	12	—	—
L.M.G.'s	18	17	29	8	363	74	296	18
Hy. M.G.'s	—	—	—	—	—	—	70	—
150 mm. Inf. Gun	—	—	—	—	—	—	4	—
75 mm. Guns...	—	—	—	—	30	2	18	—
50 mm. A.-Tk. Guns... ...	18	—	—	—	96	—	—	—
37 mm. Guns...	12	—	—	9	—	3	15	—
20 mm. Super Hy. M.G.'s ...	—	—	—	24	65	48	—	—
150 mm. Hows.	—	—	—	—	—	—	—	12
105 mm. Gun-Hows. ...	—	—	—	—	—	—	—	24
50 mm. Mortars	—	—	—	—	—	3	45	—
81 mm. Mortars	—	—	—	—	—	—	30	—

Anti-Tank Weapons and their characteristics.

Weapon.	Most effective Range.	Penetration.	Rate of Fire, Practical.	Traverse.	To Whom Issued (inch type of Tanks).	Muzzle Velocity.	Approximate Weight of Missile.	Weight of Gun.	Notes.
A.-Tk. Gun, Q.F. 50 mm.	600 yds. and under	71 mm. at 600 yds. at 30°.	—	60°	A.-Tk. Bn	2,500 ft. per sec.	1.65 lbs.	748 lbs.	Fires normal AP., A.P. 40, or H.E. Shell. Carried on lorry or towed on own wheels.
A.-Tk. Gun, 37 mm.	175 yds.	37 mm. at 600 yds. at normal. 25 mm. at 800 yds. at 30°.	8-10 r.p.m.	58°	Old Pz. K.w. III. and T.N.H.P A.-Tk. Coy. of Inf. Regt. A.-Tk. Bn. Hy. Sqn. of Recce. Units. Hy. Coy. of Lorried Inf. Bde.	2,620 ft. per sec.	5¼ ozs.	900 lbs.	Fires A.P., A.P. incendiary or H.E. Shell. M.T. drawn or on S.P. mounting.
A.A./A.-Tk. M.G., 20 mm., Super heavy.	300 yds. and under.	40 mm. at 100 yds. at normal. 18 mm. at 200 yds. at 20°.	120-150 r.p.m.	360° on cross-mounting. 10° on wheels	Armoured Cars. Pz. Kw. II. A.A. M.G. Bn. A.-Tk. Bn. A.-Tk Coy of Inf. Regt. Arty. Regt.	2,700 ft. per sec.	20 lbs.	4.9 tons	Fires A.P. with fuse at base, H.E. with percussion fuse, or H.E. with time fuse. M.T. drawn or on S.P. mounting (for ground targets only).
A.A./A.-Tk. Gun, 88 mm. (Flak. 18).	1,000 yds. and under.	100 mm. at 400 yds. at 30°. 70 mm. at 3,750 yds. at normal.	10-15 r.p.m.	360°	Hy. A.-Tk Bns.	2,700 ft. per sec.	20 lbs.	4.9 tons	
50 mm. Tank Gun...	—	63 mm. at 200 yds. at 30°. 56 mm. at 420 yds. at 30°.	—	360°	Pz. Kw III	2,600 ft. per sec.	4½ lbs.	—	Fires A.P. Shell with fuse at base and tracer, A.P. 40 or H.E. Shell.
A.-Tk. Gun, S.P M. 38 (Skoda) 47 mm.	400 yds. and under	60 mm. at 220 yds. at 30°.	8-10 r.p.m.	50°	A.-Tk Bn.	3,000 ft per sec	3½ lbs	7½ tons	Fires A.P. Shell with fuse at base and tracer, A.P. 40 or H.E. Shell. S.P. mounting (Pz. Kw.I. Tank with normal turret removed and a special superstructure fitted).
A.-Tk. Gun, Model 41, 20 mm.	Under 300 yds.	76.2 mm. at 100 yds. at normal. 60 mm. at 200 yds. at 30°. 50 mm. at 300 yds.	8-10	90°	—	4,500 ft. per sec.	1¾ ozs	600 lbs.	Fires A.P. 40 or H.E. Normally towed on trailer. May be transported by air.
A.-Tk. Rifle 39, 7.9 mm.	Under 300 yds.	30 mm. at 100 yds. at normal. 22 mm. at 200 yds. at normal.	6-8 r.p.m.	—	Rifle Coys.	3,900 ft. per sec.	¼ oz.	28 lbs.	Fires A.P. or A.P. lachrymatory bullet
A.-Tk. Rifle (Polish), 7.9 mm.	Under 300 yds.	—	6-8 r.p.m.	—	—	—	—	—	
Tk. Gun, 75 mm. ...	—	55 mm. at 400 yds. at 30°.	—	360°	Pz. Kw. IV.	1,600 ft. per sec.	15½ lbs.	670 lbs.	Fires A.P. Shell with fuse at base and tracer. H.E. or Smoke Shell.
50 mm. A.-Tk. Gun, M./38.	—	79 mm. tank armour at 600 yds. at 30°. 71 mm. ditto. 63 mm. tank armour at 800 yds. at 30°.	—	—	—	3,000 ft. per sec.	4½ lbs.	2,000 lbs	Fires A.P. Shell with fuse at base and tracer, A.P. 40 or H.E. Shell. Towed on own wheels.

LONG BARREL ANTI-TANK GUN 50 mm. CALIBRE

Characteristics of Captured Guns that may be used by the German Army.

Type.	Calibre.	Country of Origin.	Approx. Weight of Shell in Lbs.	Approx. Length of Barrel in Ft.	Approx. Muzzle Velocity in Ft. per Sec.	Maximum Range in Yards.	Traverse Degrees.	Elevation Degrees.	Depression Degrees.	Approx. Weight in Action in Tons.
Mountain Gun ... ... (Schneider M. 19).	7.5 cm.	Poland.	14	3.28	1,300	9,500	10	40	10	.687
Mountain Gun	7.5 cm.	France.	14	3.28	1,300	9,500	10	40	10	.687
Howitzer (Bofors) ...	10.5 cm.	Holland.	31	7.5	1,550	11,500	8	45	5	1.65
Howitzer	10.5 cm.	France.	35	5.85	1,450	11,000	53	50	6	1.5
Howitzer (M. 31) ...	22 cm.	Poland.	—	—	—	14,750	—	—	—	12.5
Howitzer	15.5 cm.	France.	95	5.75	1,500	12,500	6	42	0	3.35
Field Gun	7.5 cm.	France.	13	7.5	2,050	14,000	6	18	11	1.25
Field Gun (French, 1913 Model).	10.5 cm.	Poland.	35	7.5	1,800	13,500	6	37	0	2.35
Railway Gun ...	24 cm.	France.	360	24.5	2,750	26,000	360	35	0	140
Field Gun (Skoda, 1914)	10 cm.	Poland.	35	—	—	11,000	5	48	8	2.25
Railway Gun	34 cm.	France.	980	48	2,850	36,500	—	37	—	270
Gun (Bofors)	10.5 cm.	Holland.	35	13.75	2,450	18,500	60	45	3	3.5
G.P.F. Gun	15.5 cm.	France.	95	15.15	2,400	21,500	60	35	0	11.25
Railway Gun	40 cm.	France.	2,000	29	1,750	17,500	12	65	—	140
Railway Gun	28 cm.	Belgium.	290	—	—	35,000	2.15	45	0	150
Gun	22 cm.	France.	225	20	2,500	25,000	21	37	—	22
Gun (Schneider) ...	10.5 cm.	France.	35	13	2,400	19,000	50	43	0	3.5
Railway Gun	37 cm.	France.	1,550	34.5	1,900	24,500	—	40	—	250
Railway Gun	30.5 cm	France.	700	30	2,800	37,000	—	38	—	180

MEDIUM LONG BARREL GUN 105mm. CALIBRE FIRES SHELL OF 35 lbs. FOR A DISTANCE OF 19,500 YDS. THIS IS STANDARD ARTILLERY EQUIPMENT

Assault and Infantry Guns and Mortars.

	Weight in use.	Muzzle. velocity	Weight of Missile.	Speed of Fire (Max.).	Range (Max.).	Notes.
75 mm. Assault Gun	—	1,600 f.s.	14 lbs.	—	9,000 yds.	This is the 7.5 cm. Tank Gun mounted on Pz. Kw. III. chassis. Fires A.P., H.E. and Smoke Shell.
150 mm. Assault Gun	—	—	80 lbs.	—	6,000 yds.	This is the heavy Infantry Gun on a Pz. Kw. I. chassis.
150 mm. Inf. Gun ...	1.5 tons	—	80 lbs.	—	6,000 yds.	
75 mm. Inf. Gun ...	780 lbs.	750 f.s. 690 f.s.	12 lbs. 13.2 lbs.	15-20 r.p.m.	3,860 yds. 3,775 yds.	Elevation : 72°. Depression : 10°. Traverse : 12°.
50 mm. Mortar (l. Gr. W. 36).	31 lbs.	260 f.s.	2¼ lbs.	45 r.p.m.	515 yds.	One charge only. Effective range 490 yds.
81 mm. Mortar (S. Gr. W. 34).	125 lbs.	500 f.s.	7.75 lbs.	45 r.p.m.	2,080 yds.	Four charges. Effective range 1,312 yds.

LIGHT ANTI-TANK GUN 37mm. CALIBRE FIRES
1½lb. SHELL FOR A DISTANCE OF 4.000 YDS.

Anti-Aircraft Guns.

	Weight in use.	Muzzle Velocity.	Horizontal Range (Max.).	Effective Ceiling (Max.).	Vertical Range (Max.).	Weight of Missile.	Time of Flight to effective Ceiling.	Rate of Fire. In Theory. r.p.m.	Practical. r.p.m.
88 mm. Heavy A.A. Gun, Flak 18.	4.9 tons.	2,700 f.s.	16,000 yds.	34,500 ft.	34,500 ft.	20 lbs.	Approximately 6 secs. to 12,000 ft.	25	15-20
37 mm. Light A.A. Gun, Flak 36.	1½ tons.	2,700 f.s.	7,080 yds.	13,750 ft.	15,750 ft.	1,400 lbs.	14 secs.	140	60
20 mm. Light A.A. Gun, Flak 30.	990 lbs.	2,950 f.s.	5,200 yds.	7,200 ft.	12,000 ft.	¼ lb.	6 secs.	280	120

NOTES.

Krupp, 1934. Standard heavy mobile A.A. Gun. Very good A.-Tk. Gun.

Dual purpose A.A. and A.-Tk. Gun. M.T. drawn or on S.P. mounting.

Dual purpose A.A. and A.-Tk. Gun.

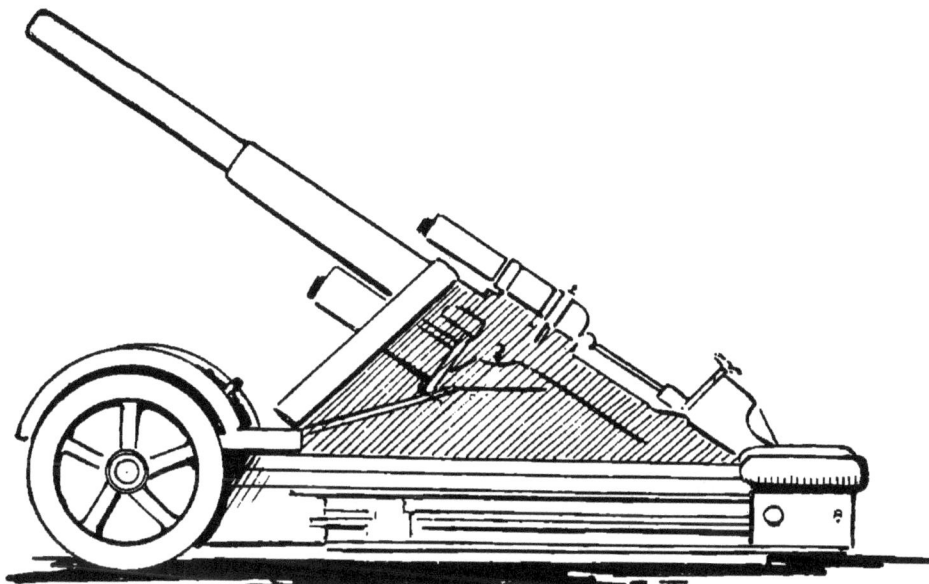

HEAVY HOWITZER 210 mm. CALIBRE FIRES
260 lb. SHELL TO A DISTANCE OF 18000 YDS.

German Small Arms Ammunition.

Type	Ball. Machine Carbines and Pistols.	A.P. (extra hard core).	A.P.T. (for A.T. Rifle).	A.P.T.	A.P.	A.P.I.	Ball.	Incendiary (fused).
Calibre	9 mm.	7.92 mm.	7.92 mm.	7.92 mm.	7.92 mm.	7.92 mm.	7.92 mm.	7.92 mm.
Colour of Cap, or annulus.	Black annulus.	(a) Red cap. (b) Red annulus.	Red annulus.	Red annulus.	Red annulus.	Black annulus.	Green annulus.	Black annulus.
Colour of Projectile	Plain.	(a) Plain. (b) Painted black.	Black tip.	Plain, with black tip.	Plain.	Plain.	Plain.	(a) Black with plain tip. (b) Plain with chromium-plated tip.
Description of Bullet.	Lead core in coated steel envelope.	Tungsten carbide core, lead sleeve, coated steel envelope.	Tungsten carbide core, lead sleeve, coated steel envelope with tracer.	Steel core, lead sleeve, coated steel envelope with tracer.	Steel core, lead sleeve, coated steel envelope.	Steel core, lead sleeve, phosphorus at base, coated steel envelope.	Lead core in coated steel envelope.	Phosphorus in nose, percussion fuse in lead plug, coated steel envelope.
Remarks	—	—	13 mm. cartridge case necked down to 7.92 mm.	—	—	—	—	—

German Machine Guns and Carbines.

	Weight lbs.	Muzzle Velocity f.s.	No. of Rounds in Belt or Magazine.	Effective Range.	Maximum Range.	Usual Rate of Fire.	Maximum Rate of Fire.	Remarks.
Machine Gun. 7.92 mm. dual purpose M.G. 34.	26.5	—	50 (belt).	1,600 yards Light Mounting.	3,280 yds. 3,820 yds. on hvy. mounting	110-120 r.p.m. (L.M.G.). 300 r.p.m. (H.M.G.).	800-900 r.p.m.	May be used as L.M.G. or H.M.G., according to mounting. Barrel changed after 250 rounds constant fire. Two or more belts can be joined end to end.
Machine Carbine. 9 mm. M.P. 38.	9.0	1,260	32 (Mag.).	Short ranges less than 300 yds.	—	80-90 r.p.m. (Fired in short bursts).	520-540 r.p.m.	Originally designed for use by parachute troops but now in general use. Six magazines carried in haversack.

MEDIUM GUN-HOWITZER 105mm. CALIBRE FIRES
32 lb. SHELL TO A DISTANCE OF 11750 YDS.

Artillery Division Weapons.

	Weight In use.	Maximum Range.	Muzzle Velocity.	Weight of Shell.	Degrees Traverse.	Degrees Elevation.	Degrees Depression.	Notes.
10 cm. Gun/How. (L.F.H. 18).	1.9 tons.	11,600 yds.	1,550 f.s.	33 lbs.	55°	40°	6°	Standard Field Gun or Howitzer.
15 cm. How. ... (S.F.H. 18).	4½ tons.	16,500 yds.	1,950 f.s.	96 lb.	60°	50°	3°	Standard Medium Howitzer.

Strength and Equipment of a Mechanized Engineer Battalion attached to a Motorized Infantry Division.

PERSONNEL AND WEAPONS.

	L.M.G.	Small Flame Throwers.	Hand Grenades.	Smoke Generators.	Large Flame Throwers.	Horse-drawn Vehicles.	Motor Vehicles.	Horses.	M.C.	Officers.	O.R.'s
Bn. H.Q.	—	—	—	—	—	—	19	—	9	7	64
Lt. Eng. Coln. ...	—	6	480	325	3	—	16	—	7	3	65
Hy. Mech. Coy. (3)	9	—	190	155	—	—	21	—	12	4	203
Br. Coln. B. ...	—	—	—	—	—	—	35	—	7	2	100

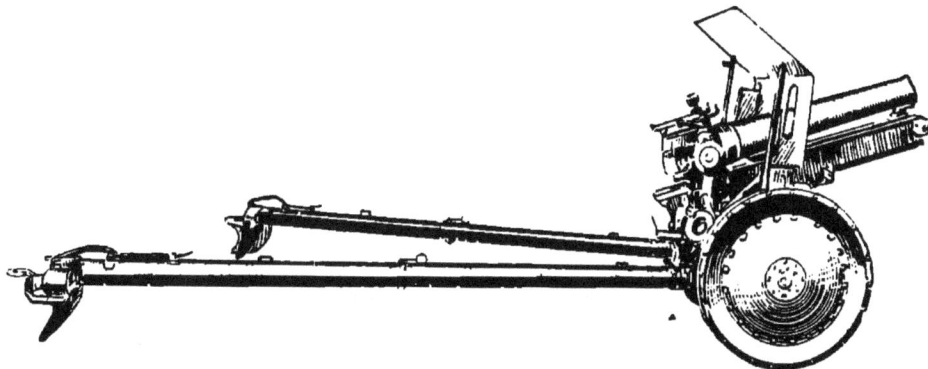

GERMAN 75mm. INFANTRY GUN FIRES 14lb. OR 10lb.
SHELL FOR AVERAGE MAXIMUM RANGE OF 5000YDS.

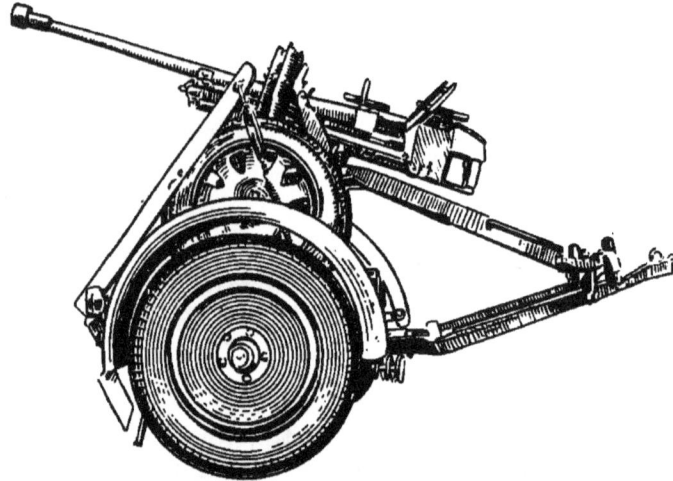

GERMAN MODEL 41 20mm.ANTI-TANK GUN

Equipment and Strength of a Mountain Engineering Battalion in a Mountain Division.
PERSONNEL AND WEAPONS.

	L.M.G.	Small Flame Throwers.	Hand Grenades.	Smoke Generators.	Medium Flame Throwers.	Horse-drawn Vehicles.	Motor Vehicles.	Horses.	M.C.	Officers.	O.R.'s
Bn. H.Q. ...	—	—	—	—	—	8	4	44	7	7	106
Lt. Mech. Coy. ...	9	—	190	155	—	—	35	—	18	4	206
Mtn. Eng. Coy. (2)	9	—	190	155	—	28	1	106	2	4	273
Lt. Mtn. Eng. Coln.	—	6	480	325	3	—	20	—	7	2	68
Br. Coln. (B.) ...	—	—	—	—	—	—	35	—	7	2	100

Equipment of Engineers (Mountain Division).

	Sandbags.	Barbed Wire (Concertina Rolls).	Drilling Equipment Sets.	Large Compressors.	Small Compressors.	Tellermines.	Exploders.	S. Mines.	Mine Detectors.	Power Saws.	16-ton Ramps.	Hand Searchlights.	Welding Equipment Sets.	Instantaneous Fuse, yards.	Plain Wire (Concertina Rolls).	Demolition Stores, lb.	Large Pneumatic Boats.	Small Pneumatic Boats.
Lt. Mech. Coy. ...	675	—	3	—	3	308	9	—	10	9	—	—	—	815	95	2,380	3	4
Mtn. Eng. Coy. (2)	200	—	3	—	3	40	6	—	10	6	—	—	1	328	40	1,050	2	6
Lt. Mtn. Eng. Coln.	600	66	2	2	—	300	2	390	—	2	—	10	3	1,635	100	2,790	—	—
Br. Coln. B. ...	—	—	—	—	—	—	—	—	—	8	—	—	—	—	12	—	24	48

Equipment and Strength of an Engineer Battalion in an Infantry Division.

PERSONNEL AND WEAPONS.

	L.M.G.	Small Flame Throwers.	Hand Grenades.	Smoke Generators.	Medium Flame Throwers.	Horse-drawn Vehicles.	Motor Vehicles.	Horses.	M.C.	Officers.	O.R.'s
Bn. H.Q.... ...	—	—	—	—	—	3	3	10	7	5	36
Hy. Mech. Coy....	9	—	190	155	—	—	21	—	12	4	205
Partly Mech. Coy.(2)	9	—	190	155	—	8	6	21	5	4	187
Lt. Eng. Coln. ...	—	6	480	325	3	—	16	—	7	3	65
Br. Coln. B. ...	—	—	—	—	—	—	35	—	7	2	100

Equipment of Engineers (Infantry Division).

	Sandbags.	Barbed Wire (Concertina Rolls).	Drilling Equipment Sets.	Large Compressors.	Small Compressors.	Tellermines.	Exploders.	S. Mines.	Mine Detectors.	Power Saws.	16-ton Ramps.	Hand Searchlights.	Welding Equipment Sets.	Instantaneous Fuze, yards.	Plain Wire (Concertina Rolls).	Demolition Stores, lb.	Large Pneumatic Boats.	Small Pneumatic Boats.
Hy. Mech. Coy....	600	—	3	—	3	295	9	—	10	9	...	--	—	650	76	2,090	3	4
Partly Mech. Coy.(2)	200	—	2	2	—	40	6	—	10	6	...	--	2	325	42	1,050	4	6
Lt. Eng. Coln. ...	600	66	2	2	—	600	2	620	—	2	—	10	3	1,635	100	2,790	—	—
Br. Coln. B. ...	—	—	—	—	—	—	—	—	—	—	8	—	—	—	12	—	24	48

TRAINING MANUALS, TEXT BOOKS AND INSTRUCTIONS

The backbone of all successful armies is its training and tactics. The Naval and Military Press publishes many such manuals of instruction – all perviously long out of print . So, whether your interest lies in the infantry and cavalry tactics of the earliest regiments of the British army in the 18th century, or the weapons manuals and firing instructions of 20th century warfare, the Naval and Military Press has the right book for you.

www.naval-military-press.com

MINES AND BOOBY TRAPS 1943

This is a War Office pamphlet, issued mid-war, in 1943. Its purpose is to introduce sappers to mines commonly used by the British Army – and how to deal with similar devices set by the Germans. The devices described and illustrated cover British anti-tank; grenade; shrapnel and assorted booby trap switches. Enemy mines are covered in chapter 2 with anti-tank, Teller mine types; French anti-tank; Hungarian; anti-personnel German and Italian; and igniters.This is a concise but comprehensive guide for British Army sappers in the art of demining or mine clearance.

9781474539395

THE .303 LEWIS GUN

Illustrated with good clear line drawings this 1941 weapon guide tells the Home Guard Volunteer how to use the 303 Lewis Gun effectively against the invading enemy.A reprint of an original handbook for the .303 Lewis Gun, that was first published in 1941. This book is a practical guide to the handling and maintenance of this iconic weapon.In the crisis following the Fall of France, where a large part of the British Army's equipment had been lost up to and at Dunkirk, stocks of Lewis guns in both .303 and .30-06 were hurriedly pressed back into service, primarily for Home Guard use. Full of fascinating information, this book taught the user the guns capabilities and all he needed to know about maintenance and combat use. Number 2 in the wartime Nicholson & Watson "Know Your Weapons" series, that offer all the important information in a more vivid style than an official publication. Illustrated with good clear line drawings.

9781474539456

ANTI-TANK WEAPONS
Smash The Tank

An insight into the amateur side of World War 2. Diagrams illustrate the main points and the devices, such as the Thermos Bomb;Phosrhorus Bomb;Sticky Bombs; that could be cobbled together from household items are described.This pamphlet was available to the Home Guard and describes the German tank and how to destroy it. It is an early War publication c1940, dealing with the light tanks used by the Germans, also the author gives examples of anti-tank actions in the Spanish Civil War, in which he took part. I'ts is a fascinating look at the "enthusiastic" approach to killing tanks.

9781474539449

TANK HUNTING AND DESTRUCTION 1940

The stated object for the distributing of this War Office manual was as "A guide and help to troops who have the determination and nerve to destroy tanks at close quarters". Intended for fighting on home soil after the very real possibility of a full German invasion, "Operation Sea Lion", this is a remarkable if somewhat naive snap shot of Britain state of preparedness,in her most dangerous hour.
The contents details Tank hunting, Tank characteristics,Tactical action,Road blocks,ambushes Ect,also includes an interesting appendix on Molotov Cocktails, and materials on other ways to destroy tanks.

9781474539401

TROOP TRAINING FOR LIGHT TANK TROOPS NOVEMBER 1939

Very early War tactics pertaining to various aspects of training with and employing armour in the British Army. Covering in concise detail that which a Light tank crew needed to know to be effective in action.
In the early years of the war, Germany held the initiative. German forces used Blitzkrieg tactics in France in 1940, making full use of the speed and armour of tanks to break through enemy defences. It was clear that German tank tactics had evolved during the inter-war period. By contrast, Britain and the Allies were playing catch-up.

9781474539302

JAPANESE WEAPONS ILLUSTRATED
September 1944

This period 'Restricted' laced binding manual was intended to be an aid to the identification of Japanese Army equipment, with sections covering: Tanks, both two-man, Tankette, light and medium; Armoured Cars; Self-Propelled Guns; Anti-Tank Guns; Artillery; Anti-Aircraft Guns; Mortars & Grenade Dischargers; Small Arms; Flamethrowers etc. Produced one year before the surrender of Japan, this work gives a good overview of the weapons the allies would find, fighting an army that despite being on the back foot, was still capable of stiff resistance in an almost entirely defensive role.

9781474539432

NOTES ON THE GERMAN ARMY-WAR
December 1940

An early war 393-page 'Notes' periodical manual from December 1940. It is a detailed review, for use in the field. The manual looks at every aspect of the "Blitzkrieg" German Army (and, to some extent, the Air Force) and gives details as known at the time. It covers the fighting arms and the services behind them – tactics, organisation, weapons and equipment. It usefully also includes a colour section on uniforms and insignia, a black-and-white plate section of small arms, infantry support and anti-tank weapons, artillery and AFVs. A series of pull-outs related to the text covering tanks etc. are also reproduced. This is an important first-class picture of the complex fighting machine that was the German Army at the end of the campaigns of 1940, only six months before the invasion of Russia.

9781474539203

GERMAN MINES AND TRAPS

Mid-1940 War Office manual with details of German mines, both the Teller and S-mine (Bouncing Betty) are covered, with techniques for disarming. Good clear full-page line drawings give both practical and technical information. Highly recommended because of the illustrations, which show how these devices worked and the components.

9781474535809

NOTES ON ENEMY ARMY IDENTIFICATIONS ITALY
October 1941

This period handbook was published to give British military personnel a better understanding of the principal characteristics of both the Italian army and the Black Shirt Militia under active service conditions , it is dated October 1941.
It begins with a description of distinctive branches, or specialities, the most characteristic of which was the arm of the Royal Carabinieri, a semi-military body occupying, historically, the senior position in the Army. Other specialities included the Grenadiers of Sardinia, the Bersaglieri, the Alpini and the San Marco Marine Regiment
The handbook then goes on to show, in order, the organisation of Command and Staff, of formations (corps and divisions) and of the arms and services; services, supply and transportation; ranks, plates (many in colour) cover uniforms, insignia, medals and decorations; armament and equipment and a chapter on the Air Force, There are chapters on tactical doctrine and principles of employment, on permanent fortifications, camouflage and abbreviations. Finally there is a brief index.
9781474539746

MANUAL OF GUERILLA TACTICS
Specially Prepared And Based On Lessons From
The Spanish And Russian Campaigns

One of the excellent, concise Bernards Pocket Books, intended to show members of the Home Guard and the regular forces that war is not conducted in a gentlemanly way – it is kill or be killed.
9781474539463

THE OFFENSIVE OF SMALL UNITS
September 1916

This is a periodical tactical manual from 1916, it focuses on the manner in which the French organised and executed their attacks and counterattacks . Summarised from the French, it lays out the process by which to operate in attacks on the German trenches. Focused purely on the operation of infantry, the purpose of this British translation is to give small infantry units the benefit of the French experience in regard to the best methods of combat, in offensive operations.
9781474537971

TRENCH WARFARE
Notes on attack and defence, February 1915

This important period manual was published in early 1915 when hope of a quick ending to the war disappeared, and trench warfare had begun to dominate the Western Front.
The manual strives to instil an offensive spirit and gives practical examples on: Close quarter, local, methods of successful warfare, and German attacks. The salient points to gather were preparation and co-operation between artillery and infantry, and that the capture of trenches is easier than their retention. Two plates illustrating tactics complete this official publication.

9781474539807

Ministry Of Home Security
OBJECTS DROPPED FROM THE AIR 1941

An illustrated Official and confidential publication, covering the many and varied types of objects that were falling from principally German aircraft during the Second phase of the blitz, including high explosives,incendiary bombs and small arms ammunition. Complete with 8 page addendum.

9781783319541

THE MUSKETRY INSTRUCTIONS FOR THE GERMAN INFANTRY 1887
(Schiessvorshrift fur die Infanterie)
Translated for the intelligence Division War Office

Translated for the War Office by Colonel C W Bowdler Bell

A facsimile that includes the supplement for the German Infantry for 1887. Musketry exercises were intended to give the infantry instruction in shooting, to make effective use of their firearm in battle. As such the manual shows important details designed to make the infantry soldier battle-ready by the end of his first year of service. Instruction is subdivided into Preparatory exercises; Target practice; Field firing; Instructional firing; Inspection in musketry; Proving the rifle M/61.84 and revolver M/83. Many black powder weapons were still used, mainly for training purposes, up to end of the First World War.

9781783313631